Release Your Inner Badass

HOW TO BREAK THROUGH YOUR BARRIERS, FIND YOUR INNER STRENGTH AND BE THE BADASS YOU TRULY ARE! (REVISED EDITION)

Marie-anne Rouse

Unlimited Solutions, LLC

Release Your Inner Badass!

Contents

Connect with Marie-anne Rouse
www.ReleaseYourInnerBadass.com
www.MarieanneRouse.com

First Printing, 2021
Revised Edition, 2022

This book is dedicated
to all who need help in finding
their inner strength
and are looking to
release their inner badass!

You got this!

Praises from Around The World

They say that what doesn't kill you makes you stronger! This has been proven over and over again for many thousands of people as expressed by the countless stories of triumph that have emerged from seemingly endless struggles. Some must hit rock bottom before seeing any hope for a better future. Marie-anne's book will help you handle your greatest challenges and begin to uncover new opportunities to emerge with a better life.

Jordan Adler, Entrepreneur.
Author of the Amazon Best Seller, "Beach Money"

By weathering the storms of life and coming out victorious on the other end, Marie-anne Rouse has been ironically blessed with Life-Enlightening Introspective Insight which she now chooses to Vocationally share with the World. With her book "Release Your Inner Badass" by your side, and within your Attitude protecting toolbox, you too will be equipped with the Mindful & Mental armor to Live a Life pursuing the things that you Want knowing and believing that you "ARE" blessed & highly favored.

... It is my Humble Honor to have crossed paths with Marie-anne Rouse and contribute these few words in support of her latest Life Shaping masterpiece - Enjoy !!!

Nelson Beltijar
Certified Life & Executive Business Coach
www.ThePositiveDrip.com

I am so honored to know Marie-anne and see her amazing growth as a leader and embracing her badass that she has in her! She has been an amazing accountability partner and is able to commit to the intentions and goals that she has. This book just confirms that she is making all of her dreams come true and showing us what's possible! I am so proud to know you, Marie-anne!

Marilyn Lamer
Speaker, Mentor, Entrepreneur
https://linktr.ee/MarilynLamer

Marie-anne is truly a woman who walks her talk. I have known and worked with her for 11 plus years and have been inspired by her bright light, sunny and kind disposition, and goofy humor. She has had her challenges as we all have, and yet she continues to always see the bright side of life and shine that upon others. I am very grateful to call her my friend and so pleasantly surprised that with all she has committed to in her life that she has also managed to write a powerful and inspirational book! I see this as part of her service to the world by sharing what she has learned to transform her life from the inside out.

Bravo Marie-anne! I love your inner badass!

Desiree Watson
President & CEO, Hawaii Workplace
HawaiiWorkplace.com

Marie-anne is dedicated to helping you discover your true worth through her mentorship, coaching, and celebration of each of your wins. She is kind, attentive, supportive, and knows exactly how to lift your spirit. "Release your Inner Badass" is sure to be an excellent read. I love that Marie-anne is sharing her story and methods you can implement to take control of your life.

Nichelle C. Davidson,
Live Well with Nichelle
https://linktr.ee/nichelle_davidson

Marie-anne Rouse is a heart-centered, raw, intuitive, loyal leader. She's unique, deep and a world impact maker! She is a great influencer that talently intertwines powerful stories with lessons. Her words of healing will impact this world. Words can't express how much she means to me and this world.

Claire Niibu-Akau
Biz Coach Claire
bizcoachclaire.com

As gold is purified in the heart of the fire, we go through trials to awaken the greatness "The Inner Badass" in us. Marie-anne went through her fire, setbacks, and challenges. But not only did she come out as pure gold, but she also brought with her golden nuggets that she graciously shared in the pages of this book to help you Release Your Inner Badass.

Odaine Mills,
Entrepreneur, Author, Transformational Coach

My relationship with Marie-anne started in an accountability group online. Her caring, authentic, and genuine personality is consistent; electronically, in person, and in these pages. She is truly a person that blesses everyone she knows!

When we eventually met face to face at a convention, a sisterhood was formed that feels like it was meant to be. She has since been a mentor, cheerleader, teacher, teammate, and inspiration to me from across the ocean. I am thrilled to experience her creativity, leadership, dedication, and friendship because she calls out the best version of me.

Her book is a staple in my professional and personal development collection. My plan is to gift it to each new business associate who joins our team so they can gain strength for the journey of pursuing their dreams from the examples shared!

Nicole J. Nohl,
Founding Director
"Making Penny Memories" Foundation

Once you learn how to Master the Art of Human Connections you attract an abundance of opportunities, referrals, friends, and love into your life. However, it starts from within you first and it's people like Marie-anne and books like "Release Your Inner Badass" that give us the vision to see it and steps to make it happen.

Darla DiGrandi-Aguilera
CEO of Master the Art of Human Connections
Serial Entrepreneur, Author, Speaker
www.DarlaD.com

I have had the distinct honor and privilege of being a co-author with Marie-anne in the book Resilience to Greatness. She brings much light to this world through her life experiences.

She teaches us nothing can dim the light that shines from within. No matter where you go, no matter what the weather ALWAYS bring your own sunshine!!

Shlomo Nash
International entrepreneur health and wellness.
Strive for Excellence Global
strive4excellenceglobal.org

Some people "talk the talk" others, "walk the walk'. The ones who "walk" are who I listen to. Marie-anne Rouse is one of those people. Les Brown, my mentor says, "When life knocks you down, try to land on your back. Because if you can look up, you can get up".

This quote explains Marie-anne perfectly. Life has knocked her down many times. Every time, she got back up! The book you hold in your hands, comes right from the pages of Marie-anne's life. This means Marie-anne will teach you to navigate life's storms and Thrive.

Thank you SO Much Marie-anne Rouse for being such an example and for walking the walk.

Pamela Henkel
Pastor, Success Coach, and Author
That would be fantastic..
www. Purposewithpamela.com

This dynamic book will change how you look at life and the way you deal with its hardships. Chock Full of powerful lessons to inspire, encourage and give you the hope to blaze your road to success.

Susan Friedmann
CSP, international bestselling author of
Riches in Niches: How to Make it BIG in a small Market

I've had the privilege to work with Marie-anne as co-authors on a recent book project. Hearing her personal story immediately grabbed my attention. I appreciate her three important truths: you are stronger than you realize; family & relationships are priorities, and we must take care of ourselves before we can truly take care of others. She is truly a resilient woman and transformational leader that can and will help you find your inner strengths. I have no doubt that this book will get you through those barriers that have been holding you back and launch you into a whole new world of greatness!!

Neco Johnson Sr.
Master Life Coach & Leadership Consultant
necojohnson.com

This book "Release Your Inner Badass" spoke to me. If you are looking for a book that will turn your fears into greater success, then I recommend this book. It confirmed so much of my personal experience (finding the inner strength in darkest moments), offered new ways of seeing/experiencing aspects of my life (choosing to move forward in spite of challenges), and provided inspiration in a gentle and powerful way (Passion/Purpose, Intention, Embracing Abundance). The sky is no longer the limit, but our point of view, so let's all RISE TO GREATER HEIGHTS!

Real N. Kunene - CTC, SAM, TCP
RISE TO GREATER HEIGHTS NETWORK
RiseToGreaterHeights.com

I had the honor to meet Marie-anne in 2020 through my transformational and business coach Biz Coach Claire who thought that meeting Marie-anne would help me with my business survive an unpredictable year by pivoting and focusing on client retention. Little did I know at the time... I was going to meet one of the most amazing and genuine women I know today... not to mention, I also gained a life-long friend! The title alone "Release Your Inner Badass" ' I feel is Marie-anne speaking to us all as she motivates and inspires other people to be the best at our best! Thank you for sharing your knowledge and maintaining your work ethic. You are a great role- model to all young women inspiring to motivate others to also release their inner badass!

Leilani U. Soliven
Medicare Specialist
pbchawaii.com/lani

Do you want to be happy no matter what has happened to you in your past? Marie-anne is living proof with bucket loads of evidence that it is possible. To live a life that you not only enjoy but one that you design and create yourself. Follow her guidance into the abundant life that is waiting for you. Just Jump!

Melissa Burnside
Varsity Coach, Published Author, Global Speaker
Coachburnside.com

Thank You - Merci - Mahalo

My husband....... who has always been there for me, believed in me and encouraged me to follow my heart. My biggest fan. The man who listens to all my ramblings and eclectic ideas. The man who made my heart pitter-patter back when I was 18 and to this day.

My children..... Joseph, Jacob, and Sarah inspire me and are a BIG part of my why. My heart is filled with joy seeing you explore what your talents are. You are a treasure and a gift.

My mom...... gave me the gift of life and always told me that it didn't matter what I did as a profession as long as I was happy from within. She would say that even if flipping burgers is what made me happy, she'd be happy for me. Keep in mind I was already vegetarian when she would tell me that.

My siblings......whom I have learned many life lessons from and will always have my love no matter how far apart we are. We are literally spread out around the world.

My bestie.....the sister from another mother, the ying to my yang. It doesn't matter how long we are apart, anytime we get together it is as if no time has passed.

The Hualalai Ohana Foundation for providing support over the years in many ways helping to make some of my dreams into realities.

Those who have been mentors, guiding lights, and encouragers in my life......**Joann Seery, Biz Coach Claire, Desiree Watson, Nicole Nohl, Jordan Adler, Darla DiGrandi-Aguilera, Les Brown, Jon Talarico, Patrick Snow, Lynn Howard, Marilyn Lamer, Nichelle Davidson, Ellen Marrs, Wendy Hoggatt, Christina Estrada, Leilani Kailiawa, Arliss Dudley-Cash** and that is just the tip of the iceberg.

My High School English as a Second Language Teacher and now friend........**Nancy Schwalen**. Treasuring all the memories created.

My High School English teacher who taught me to use the word "plethora" ....**William Rasmussen**. And guess what? I am going to be writing for a plethora of books.

My first publisher......**Susan Friedman** for her encouragement and guidance for this book.

The support and encouragement I have received from my Ohana & extended Ohana in **Greener Still, Send Out Cards, Shaklee, and BNI**.

The many speakers and authors I have had the pleasure to collaborate with both on stage and in published books.......**Nompumelelo Real Kunene, Pamela Henkel, Elke Preuß, Neco Johnson, Melissa Burnside, Joanna Bricker Kleier, Debbie Halbrook, Grant Raphael, Kyle Spyrides, Shlomo Nash, Michelle Borel, Alieu Bah, Odaine Mills, Nelson Beltijan, Erin Baer**, and more!

The Badass Women in the **Femillionaire Club**....you know who you are!

Foreword

One thing I have learned in life is to never make assumptions of the people you meet. You never fully appreciate a person for who they truly are until you invest in that relationship and understand where they came from and what brought them to where they are today. Marie-anne is one of those people.

I have known Marie-anne Rouse for almost 12 years. I first met her at a networking meeting. She immediately struck me as a positive, happy person with a passion for health. That was obvious to me from the first time I met her. What I did not know was the journey she was on to be authentically the person she wanted to be. As I grew to know her better, I witnessed her transformation. I also realized her strength, courage and inner badass were traits that I would admire and depend on to help me personally and professionally.

We have all met that person. That business owner, the neighbor that seems to have everything. The person who makes life and business look easy. What we do not see are the struggles, the sacrifices, the self-doubt, the decisions that needed to be made daily to get to where they were going. It is with Marie-anne's honesty and commitment to be her true self that I gained a friend, a business associate, and a support system.

Sharing how others have overcome their challenges and grew into the person they are gives us the green light for everyone to be themselves. Marie-anne will share powerful stories of personal challenges and lessons she encountered through the years that allowed her to make decisions that were hers alone. She shares what she learned over the years, coaching tips, success stories supported by motivational quotes, tips and scientific facts.

Just when you think you have learned all of life's lessons or have encountered every experience that is meant for you, there is more. Learning and growing is a lifelong process no matter how old or wise you are. Marie-anne has not stopped learning or developing. Her growth continues to give us the guidance and mentorship for our continued evolution. I am grateful for knowing Marie-anne and having her be an important part of my life. I am sure after you read this book, you will understand why. I am hoping that you are inspired by Marie-anne's stories and bravery. The insight, resources, and knowledge you need to release your inner badass is just a fingertip away!

Joann Seery
Serious Business Solutions
seriousbusinesssolutions.info

Introduction

The initial title for this book was *"The Reluctant Runner"* which is the start of the story behind how this book was birthed along with the stories that emerged (and some resurfaced) in the process that I am going to be sharing with you on these pages. This book got started at 5 am one Sunday morning as my husband and I were getting ready to go out for a training session. We were training to run together.....the Honolulu Marathon 2020!

Was I a runner when I started this book?

Ha! No! Far from it.

Actually, the first day I went out training with my husband, I agreed that I would pick up my pace and he agreed that he would slow down his. In a way, we planned on meeting each other halfway with adjusting our pace. Well, while picking up my pace, he was still running circles around me. And I do mean that literally, yes, he was running circles around me which was pretty funny .... at first.

Am I a runner now? Well, you can decide for yourself as you read through the few stories from this adventure we embarked on together.

The journey to run the Honolulu Marathon 2020 was quite an adventure, to say the least. I recorded many stories on the voice recording app of my cell phone while I was out for my training sessions. I recorded about life events, overcoming struggles, and finding my own inner strength......and what were ways that I discovered that inner strength even when I didn't think I had anything left.

Is this a book about running stories? Well, there will be just a few that relate to a couple of experiences that came up while training and the actual Marathon day, which ended up being virtual due to all the Covid craziness we all got to experience. Some of the stories are deep and heavy but keep in mind that I am writing this book today about finding that inner strength that helped me through those life events. Some stories will probably keep you on the edge of your seat as you read through to find out the outcome and some may have you laughing along with me at my personal mishaps and discoveries.

I will be sharing those stories as there may be golden nuggets in those experiences that will help you in your journey to find your own inner strength. While my experiences are different from yours in many ways, and possibly similar in others, I know without a doubt that you are stronger than you even realize at this very moment. No matter what is going on in your life, or how big of a struggle you are currently experiencing, I know that you have the strength within you that you have not tapped into yet and my intention is to be a lighthouse in whatever storm you may be going through...right now.

Being that this is a revised edition, you might be wondering what has changed. My initial thought was just to add a section with some powerful 2-minute journaling questions. These questions have been powerful even in creating conversations that rolled into deep, heartfelt conversations. Then, there was an error with a date that did not affect the story but it was an error just the same. It was something that only my husband and my bestie would know to be a mistake and they both caught it. Not the type of error to make a whole revised version for but since I was making changes, I took advantage of the situation to make the correction. The last change had to do with the style and size to bring costs down and to make it easier to carry anywhere you go. The first time around, I wanted it to have a hardcover with a dust jacket, partially out of my own vanity. I really wanted that look and feel in your hands. There were also certain details that were important with the inside flaps of the dust cover. The right inside flap has I AM statements for you and the left inside flap has affirmations. By going to soft cover, I am able to pass the savings onto you by bringing down the purchase price and so as not to lose those important elements, you will find them in the back section titled "Daily Reminders."

This book is written for you. I chose not to have it professionally edited because I felt it important for you to hear my true voice. I have kept it muffled for way too long and I am not about to change my voice simply because something isn't grammatically correct. I want you to know that it is okay to do something imperfectly because it means you are doing something. I want you to hear and connect with my unleashed inner badass (which, of course, means I can remove the inner part). I want to connect with your inner badass so you too can be unleashed.

So, with that said, let us dive right into our first story.

1

⁓

Giving up is not an option

My friend .....you are stronger than you realize! You can break through personal barriers and limitations. You can find your inner strength and you can release your inner badass. I may not know you but I do know something about you. I know that you were born for a very specific purpose. After all, your journey started back when you were that energy that then became that ONE microscopic sperm swimming against all odds to be the ONE and only YOU. You have already achieved and won the hardest race and accomplishment that needed to take place in order to start your very existence as we know it, the ONE who is reading these words at this very moment. You were driven then because you already knew you had a purpose as to why YOU had to be born and giving up then was not an option, just like giving up now is not an option either. No matter how deep or dark things may appear at any given time in your life, it is important for you to remember that you have already overcome the greatest odds. Your journey from energy to sperm to the very existence of you as you are now is marvelous to say the least.

I know that there are times when we don't even know how strong we are until we have no choice but to be strong. Yes, I know how it can feel like being at the end of one's rope. Yes, I know firsthand the feeling of desperation, hopelessness, and wanting to give it all up. And yes, I also know how it feels to pull oneself out of that deep, dark space and make that climb back up even when it can feel like a daunting and impossible climb.

There was a point in my life when I had no choice but to be strong. It was a time when things got so deep that I could not see the light. It was a time when things got so emotionally dark that I sat on the floor of my mother's bathroom......about to make a permanent decision based on a temporary situation that did not feel temporary to me. My mother was on the other side of that bathroom door, bedridden and unable to care for herself. My younger sister was in her own bedroom, most likely doing home-work. That very moment was the turning point in my life when I learned that yes, I am stronger than I realize. Some people have to hit rock bottom in order to rise and that, my friend, was my rock bottom.

But you know what? I had within me what it took to rise. I had it within me all along but I didn't know it until I started that long, steep climb. And you too have the strength within you, even if you don't know it at this very moment. I am here to tell you that you are stronger than you realize. Whether I liked it or not, I was being tested because of the purpose I was born for. I had a purpose I did not yet see. I had a purpose I could not have fathomed back them. But a purpose that required me to be tested to my limits so that I could be here today to share my message, to share my voice, and to speak into your life.

I have heard Mr. Les Brown say plenty of times.

No test.... No testimonies!

I sure was being tested but giving up was not in my DNA. Giving up was not an option. You may be wondering. How did I get to such a deep and dark place? You see, I was 18 years old when I got the call while at work that my mom had been in a car accident. It was a pretty bad accident and I thank the stars up above, the powers beyond what we see, that as I am typing up these words, my mother is still with us, even if we live just about a whole continent apart...which is a whole story in itself that I just might share with you too as it is one of following one's childhood dreams.

I never expected, especially at the young age of 18, to become my own mother's caregiver. It was, you could say, a life-defining situation. I have heard it said that glow sticks have to break in order to glow brighter. I was far from shining during that entire experience.

It was what was needed to get me to my breaking point. And now, I do glow brighter than I ever could! I do glow brighter than I even imagined possible back then. Reflecting back, I now understand that things happen for us instead of to us. It was crucial for me to live through that whole experience of becoming my mother's caregiver. Not only did I learn just how strong I was within but I also discovered the importance of certain relationships in my life as those relationships are the ones that were that light of hope. Those relationships were the lighthouse within my storm. Because of those relationships, I found the "why" I absolutely had to keep going. Yes, I still had the choice to give up or keep going. And yes, my "why" in that deepest and darkest moment revealed to me that I needed to find a way to make it through and that giving up was not an option. While the hope was just a tiny flicker, it was enough to take the first step out of the emotional abyss. It didn't light the whole path, just a single step. A single step at a time was all that was needed. Actually, a single step at a time was all I could do... at that time.

That tiny flicker was enough to make me want to dig really deep within me to find that hidden strength within. If I had not gone through that whole experience, I would not be the woman that I am today.

I would not be the wife that I am today.

I would not be the mother that I am today.

I would not be uncovering and unleashing the greatness that is within me.

You get the picture...... I would not be the badass I am today!

I share this with you because maybe you, or someone you know, is going through some tough times right now. I want you to remember that

You are stronger than you realize.
You can break through any barriers.
You have more strength within you than you know.
You are a badass!

No better yet. I want you to highlight, circle, and say out loud:

I am stronger than I realize.
I am breaking through barriers.
I have more strength within me than I know.
I am a badass!

Here is another way to look at it. Think of the 1964 Mary Poppins movie. If you have never seen it, it is the movie where Julie Andrews made her screen debut as an English nanny. There is something magical about her, how she travels and.....her travel carpet bag. As odd as it may sound, you are like a Mary Poppins bag, just way more stylish! Everything that you need is within you. Like Mary Poppins who needs to dig deep at times to find what she needs, sometimes you have to dig, dig, and dig just to find exactly what it is that you need. Just like Mary Poppins, sometimes what you pull out isn't what you need, so keep on digging because everything you need is already within you. While it may not always feel like a simple thing to do, keep digging because it is there. And, if you are going through a tough time right now I also want you to remember that giving up is not an option.

Whatever challenges you may be experiencing, remember that they are temporary. Quitting or giving up does not serve you or anyone else. This could very well be your own life-defining moment. Right now may be your very own life-defining situation that requires you to tap into and unleash your inner badass. And while I understand that you may not see it because of the inner turmoil, and possible chaos, of the moment, there is always a reason behind it all and somehow you have made a reservation in time to be right here, an appointment in time if you will to be here, right now. Just like you have made an appointment in time to be reading this book because there are gemstones within these pages that you need either for yourself or to share with someone else.

This event in my life that I just shared with you happened roughly 30 years ago. Some of the gemstones that came out of that experience were easy to find and right on the surface. And some were buried down so deep that it took me 30 years to realize what they were. Use my stories. Use my life's tests turned to testimonies. Use the gemstones from my experiences to close the time gap and release your inner strength.

I do understand. Even if you think that the odds are stacked way up high against you right now, remember that you fought the hardest fight of your life already back when you had to swim your fastest race. Back when you had to be the first....because there was something already within every vibration and fiber of you (yes, even as that microscopic sperm) telling you that you had to win because you are destined for something much bigger.

And if you are still not sure how you can make it through, I want you to think about being a bumblebee. I want you to erase the thought about the odds. The bumblebee doesn't know anything about odds. The bumblebee has no idea that the odds are against it. Mathematically, the bumblebee is not supposed to be able to fly! It is so heavy in comparison to its wingspan that it is mathematically.... technically.... impossible for it to fly. Picture it in your mind right now.

Tiny wings.

Big FAT butt.

And yet the bumblebee flies. And you know what, the bumblebee does not know that it's not supposed to be able to.

The bumblebee does not know that the odds are against it.

The bumblebee does not know that it is defying mathematical equations.

And yet, without fail...... the bumblebee flies.

And so no matter how big the odds are that are stacked against you. I want you to know that YOU can defy the odds because, my friend....

You are stronger than you realize.
You are breaking through barriers.
You are finding your inner strength.
And, you are releasing your inner badass.

It is true. Like I said before, I have been there. I totally understand that there are times when you may not see any possibilities. If I had seen the possibilities, you know that I would not have ended up ready to end it all. I know that there are times when it seems that all hope is lost. There are times when you may be in such despair that, you too, are ready to make that permanent decision based on a temporary situation. At that very moment, I myself didn't see it as a temporary situation. I felt like there was no hope left. I felt drained of all my physical and emotional strength.

Or so..... I thought. Yes, I was stronger than I realized and I had more strength available even in that moment when I thought it was the end. All it took.....sounds so simple "All it took." All it took was a tiny glimmer of hope. It was that tiny sparkle in a dark room to show me that I had an itsy-bitsy little bit of rope to pull me out of that abyss. It was just enough of it to start pulling me out of that despair. It was just enough to start pulling me back ever so slowly into the light and out of the darkness. I realized that this moment in my life was only a bend in the road, not the end of the road. And while that felt like an extremely sharp and abrupt bend in the road, that is exactly what it turned out just to be.....only a bend in the road. This was a time to hang on because giving up or letting go while going around that very sharp and abrupt bend.....was not an option.

After all, giving up was not in my DNA and neither is it in yours. I had not lived my life's purpose yet and neither have you. There is greatness within you and the world needs for you to share that gift that you have within, just the same as the world needs the gift that is within me.

> *"What lies behind us and what lies before us,*
> *are small matters compared to what lies within us."*
> Ralph Waldo Emerson

This brings me to another quote by Ralph Waldo Emerson:

> *" When we bring what is within us out into the world*
> *miracles happen"*

In that dark place of despair is when I started to tap into my inner strength. That was just the start. I held onto that extra little piece of rope that I realized was there to help pull me out. It was a moment when I needed to focus on that ONE small beacon to guide me out of my own personal, physical and emotional storm. Glimpses and glimmers of hope appear in different forms. For me, the beacon in my storm was the love I felt for my mom and my younger sister. I realized something quite important in that pivotal moment. I realized that all I would be doing was to transfer my struggles, amplified by grief, onto them and I knew I could not do that to them. There was no way possible in my heart that I could justify taking such drastic action. The tears just rolled down my face realizing that my younger sister would be the one who would make the discovery of the results of my actions while my mother was bedridden and recovering from injuries.

I knew I had to keep going......even if, at that moment, I knew I had to keep going just for them. The keep-going part for myself came a little bit later which could be a whole other chapter in itself. But at that moment, I felt like the frog that fell into the bucket of cream. Maybe you heard the story before. Basically, in the story, there are two frogs and they fall in a big bucket full of cream. The sides are pretty high. The first frog attempts to jump out but with no success as there is nothing for it to get a grip on to be able to climb out. That frog tries and tries to jump and as it grows frustrated and tired, the frog gives up and drowns. The second frog saw what just happened and frantically started to swim around in the cream while trying to figure out a way out. And, if you didn't know the story already, you probably guessed it. All that swimming around caused the cream to turn into butter which gave the frog a place to climb and eventually jump out of the bucket. I felt like that second frog. Stuck in a bucket of despair with sides too high for me to jump out. Giving up was not an option and so I swam and swam in "my bucket of despair" until that little glimpse of hope helped me to create something to grasp on to help me get out of the bucket. My mom eventually recovered, for the most part, from the injuries and I made plans to recharge my own batteries with more self-care and healthier food choices. What do I mean by healthier food choices? Well, while it felt good from an emotional standpoint, I am in awe that my body did as good as it did considering that I was living on chocolate! Literally, I ate a hazelnut chocolate bar a day. By the time I got that glimpse of hope, I was a 5-foot 2-inch teenager weighing a feathery 90 pounds. Better food choices started by making sure I had ONE smoothie every day even if it meant sipping on it all day long just to be able to finish it. It was a very basic, simple 4 ingredient smoothie.....a place to start.

Recharging my batteries also meant taking time for myself and going somewhere on my own once my mom was mobile enough. *Hawaii - where angels come to repair their wings* is on a wall hanging created by Dennis Gregory, poet, writer, artist, and songwriter, whom I ended up meeting years later. Hawaii, meaning the Big Island which is the one called Hawaii, is where I decided to go and repair my wings.

Now in wrapping up this chapter, let me share with you 8 things to remember when going through tough times. These are great reminders that a friend shared.

1. Everything can and will change.
2. You have overcome challenges before.
3. It's a learning experience.
4. Not getting what you want can be a blessing.

5. Allow yourself to have some fun.
6. Being kind to yourself is the best medicine.
7. Other people's negativity isn't worth worrying about.
8. And there is always, always, always, something to be Thankful for.

Now, why are those 8 things to remember so important? Very simply put,

> You are stronger than you realize.
> You are breaking through barriers.
> You are finding your inner strength.
> And, you are releasing your inner badass.

I am stronger than I realize.
I am breaking through barriers.
I have more strength within me than I know.
I am a badass!

2

ᔕᔑ

No Pity Parties Allowed

Okay, here we go. Now I'm going to share about some of those Marathon training sessions and experiences because those were times when I had a good number of opportunities to have some pity parties. Sometimes, I do say..... I did have pity parties.

Since I was out on the road, literally, let me start with a truth from Dolly Parton who brilliantly said.....

> *If you don't like the road you're walking,*
> *start paving another one.*

You see, one of the reasons why I decided to do my very first marathon was because of what a doctor had told me. He said the pain I was in was a pain I had to learn to "just live with". So the back story to this part is that I had been in an auto accident. The accident itself was minor. My car was an accordion down on one side and the reason I was personally enduring such pain is because of how I was positioned in the car, twisted, bent over at the time of the impact. I did go to the chiropractor, massage therapist, and physical therapist until the insurance company decided it was time to do an independent medical examination at which time, the Independent examiner decided I was due to get my accident medical benefits cut off. He looked at me and simply said "this is the best you're going to get and you have to learn to live with it".

Of course, I had choices. I could have a pity party and let my fears, thoughts, emotions, and beliefs paralyze me in that mindset. I could have a pity party and let the news drag me down. I could keep on feeding the pity party and feed the negativity mindset vampires suck away by giving them a straw.

I had a choice to make. I could ride the pity party train or I could say "watch me" and prove him wrong. Well, you guessed it. I decided to say..... "watch me" and prove him wrong.

It took me a good number of years before doing my very first marathon.

I walked it.

I finished it.

And..... I proved him wrong.

Over the years I have learned better ways to take care of myself. Over the years I had learned what specific movements and stretches were beneficial to me. With doing so well, at least in my own opinion, with my first marathon experience, I decided to do a second one. And this time it was a whole other experience but it was not from lack of training. It was not from a lack of stretching. It was from being in a different location and not properly preparing for that location.

During that second race.....I started having a pity party! I was one of the last ones on the course. There was just a handful of us still out on the course. The sun was very bright and hot! We were surrounded by black lava fields, which intensified the heat of the sun in the middle of the day. There was no shade out there on Queen Kaahumanu Highway. The pity party that I started having was because I was noticing the aid stations with the water and hydration we're already taken down. I was going into the mode of "woe is me" and getting upset at the volunteers who were taking down their stations when they were simply doing what they were supposed to do there.

I had a choice. I had a choice to be bitter or I had a choice to get better. And yes, at first I was bitter but then I realized the choice was mine. I could let the bitterness consume me and make my experience with this Marathon even harder. Or, I could get off that pity party train by asking myself some very simple questions.

Is this pity party serving me in any way?

Is this pity party serving anyone in any way?

Were there any benefits at all to having this pity party?

Well, you guessed it. The answer was a big fat, No! It was time for me to let go of that pity party mentality or let it drag me down. I was getting so close to that finish line. Even a couple of miles can feel long when you're doing a whole 26.2 miles. I decided at that point to put a smile on my face. Did you know that our emotions affect our health and well-being? Just a few minutes of bitterness and anger can weaken the immune system for over 4 hours! But on the opposite end of the spectrum, a few minutes of laughter can boost the immune system for over 24 hours. So here, while I was not looking to boost my immune system, I knew I needed to do something to shift my state of mind. I was simply looking to shift my thought patterns and getting myself out of that pity party.

What do you think I did? I decided to do something very simple. I decided to put a smile on my face. I do mean that literally. I forced myself to smile and think happy thoughts, which in my case works by singing songs from musicals. Guess what! Putting a smile on my face physically changed how I was moving along the course. Putting a smile on my face literally helped to put a little bit more pep in my step. Putting a smile on my face even lifted my spirit. and you want to hear the cool thing that happened..... by putting that smile on my face it helped me to tap into the inner strength that was still deeper within me. Putting that smile on my face helped me to release my inner badass and I started breaking through more barriers within my own mind and body. And even with going down the wrong ramp ....

Yes......the volunteers that guide you in which direction to go weren't there so I went down the wrong ramp and thankfully noticed fairly quickly and could turn around, go back, and re-enter the ramp...... The correct ramp that time and be on my way to the finish line. I still finished with a smile and I still finished within the allotted time. And as I slowly walked back to the hotel where I was staying, I said to myself..... never again! I was done with doing marathons. I did not want to put myself through that experience of being out there in the hot sun, getting sunburned because, yes, of all the things to forget........I forgot to pack my sunscreen. So yes, I was cooked. I was done. I had enough.

The no-sunscreen effects did bring on laughter for weeks. I was so sunburned! I was red like a lobster except for certain areas that had been covered. My shoulders for example were lobster red while my arms were a nice pasty white. This happened because I wore compression sleeves to provide sun protection and to have something I could soak with water at aid stations. But, not having sunscreen on my shoulders, or my legs, created quite a funny combo of lobster red and pasty white in unusually patterned spots. I am glad I could laugh about it, but still, I was done with marathons!

Then.......Imagine my surprise when on December 31st, 2019 just before the stroke of midnight, my husband popped the question "Will you do the Honolulu Marathon with me?" and I said yes without even batting an eye. What was I getting myself into? What did I just say? Jeepers! Training and completing the Honolulu Marathon was a whole other journey by itself. The year 2020 was the year like none of us had ever experienced. It was like the world came to an abrupt halt and chaos affected all in various ways. And, amidst all the covid craziness, just like almost all meetings, graduations, and funerals to just name a few..... the Honolulu Marathon went virtual.

As I wrote in the introduction, the thought for this book was born one Sunday morning at 5 a.m. as I was about to go for a training run.

This is now my third Marathon. I'm going to say that it is my last and I know that's exactly what I said the time before! But this third Marathon was different in many ways. This was a marathon of breaking through my own personal barriers. I don't know if you've heard the story about fleas. An experiment was done with fleas. These fleas were put inside a jar and then the lid was put on. Now you know fleas can jump really, really high, especially in comparison to their body size. If I was a flea at my size, I would be able to pole vault jump, in one jump, without a pole.... that's in comparison to size. Basically, fleas jump very high. For this experiment, all the fleas were put inside a jar and the lid closed.

The fleas were jumping and hitting the lid and you could hear the pop pop pop each time that a flea would hit the lid. And the fleas just keep on jumping..... pop .....pop...... pop and then little by little the popping sounds faded and stopped. Looking in the jar, the fleas were still jumping but they were no longer hitting the lid. The fleas learned that they could not get out of that jar. The fleas learned that there was a lid and that was their limit. But here is the interesting part about that experiment. Once the lid was removed, the fleas kept on jumping..... but they were not jumping out of the jar! They kept on jumping within their new boundaries because they got trained to stay within the limits of the lid even if the lid was no longer there.

And that is exactly what I had done to myself. I had trained myself to be inside my own jar. I had accepted other people's opinions of me. I had accepted what a doctor said of me and I had accepted what my thoughts were of my own limitations. This is also why, I believe, I said yes without batting an eye when my husband asked me if I would do the Honolulu Marathon with him.

For me training and completing that Marathon was going to be my own personal Journey of removing the lid...... of breaking the jar, not just jumping out of it.

My jar.

My lid.

My barriers.

My blocks.

My limitations.

It was time for me to break free...... physically and emotionally.

Believe me when I say that there were a good number of times during my training that I felt like having pity parties! What helped me to overcome those feelings? Once again, something very simple to do. I do realize that sometimes, the simplest things to do can be the hardest to do at times. But still, this was something very simple that I could do. What is it, you ask?

It was to think about my best friend who was going through some life-changing events, her own race you could say.... but her race had no finish line in sight. A race where she didn't know the distance. A race where she didn't know what the outcome would be. You see, my best friend was going through chemotherapy..... again. And as I was training, out there on Queen Kahanumanu highway

.... wanting to quit because I was tired.

.... wanting to quit because I was sore.

.... wanting to quit because there were no public bathrooms available anywhere.

.... wanting to quit because it was early in the morning or

.... wanting to quit because it was too hot.

.... Basically, I wanted to quit because I was having, once again, pity parties.

What helped me to stop those pity parties in their tracks, was to think about my best friend and that she did not have a choice to quit.

......She had to be stronger than she realized.

......She had to break through her own personal and emotional barriers.

....She had to find and tap into her inner strength in order to release her own badass self. By focusing on her and her journey, and how strong she was even though she did not realize it, helped me to break through. That simple, yet sometimes hard, step helped me to find more strength that helped me to be the badass that I know I am.

A lesson to learn from those moments that can easily become pity party sessions is to be thankful for those moments as you can change your mindset and use that energy to fuel your drive to break through any barriers. Just like I was doing, you can use that energy to fuel your drive to find your inner strength. You can use that energy to release your inner badass. Helen Keller, who became blind and deaf at 19 months old, said

When one door closes, another one opens

And there is a choice we get to make when facing a closed door. We can have a pity party or we can shift our mindset, and our energy, to either create a new door or simply discover that there is already another one cracked open.

As you go on your own journey, should you find yourself in a place where you are stuck in front of a door that is closed or in a jar of your own making (maybe from accepting other people's opinions of you, as I did) and you feel like having your very own pity party, remember.... no pity party allowed! Anytime you feel a pity party coming on, ask yourself:

Does a pity party serve me in any way?

Does this pity party serve others in any way?

And if the answer is no, which 99.99% of the time the answer is going to be a big fat "No!", acknowledge how you are feeling.

Let it sit for a moment then put a smile on your face and shift the energy within. Put a smile on your face because ....

You are stronger than you realize. Put a smile on your face because....

It will help you to tap into your inner strength. Put a smile on your face because

You are a badass!

If you don't like the road
you're walking,
start paving another one.
— Dolly Parton

3

⌇

The Secret Sauce is.... out of your current comfort bubble

Oh, this is going to be a fun chapter to share with you. I am about to share an adventure that, in the end...... WE KNEW we were badass! This is one of my favorite stories to share as each time I share it, I relive that action-packed morning.

Okay. Let us dive into the fun story. It is a story about, you guessed it...the secret sauce that is out of your comfort bubble....in this particular case, doing exactly what we were told not to do.

This happened in the summer of 2017 during a trip to Georgia with both my younger sister and my best friend. This was one of my regular business trips to attend a conference. Each time I travel for a conference, I love that I get to explore a different area of the country which is a fun way to explore new places. Every time I go, I always block a little extra time on my calendar to go out and have some fun, explore and do something different. Whether we've gone zip lining, gotten tattoos, touched sharks (baby ones at an aquarium), or gone line dancing, we always found something fun and exciting that we wanted to do as we explored and created memories together. On this particular trip, we decided to go "tube the 'hooch." Yes, we went tubing down the Chattahoochee River in Helen, a cute little Bavarian-like town.

Let me paint you a picture of this adventure we embarked on. Here we are, riding in a little shuttle bus similar to a small school bus with a small open-air trailer hitched to the back, filled with big green swim tubes. The van is full of other families and friends ready to have some fun. I enjoyed the view as we rode up the long windy road....the trees, a small wooden old abandoned building, and clear skies. And then, there we were, at the drop-off point. The excitement was building as we all hopped off the bus, one by one, and gathered around the back to get our tubes. These tubes were like huge inner tubes with a closed bottom so we had a place to sit "in" our tubes. During the drive up, the driver went over basic instructions and as we all grabbed our tubes, he reiterated and made a point to remind all of us that, no matter what.....we are not to get in the water, we need to stay in the tubes! The water may not be very deep, but it can get pretty rough unexpect-edly. No problem. That was an easy rule to follow. But, yes, I know.... rules are easily broken, and sometimes, we really need to break them. So yes, in this story we broke this rule, and what an adventure that was.

Just like life, we can all be on the same river, and yet we each have a different experience. A great example of that is with the three of us, my sister ended up being in outer sections where water currents were slow-moving, peaceful, and calm.   On the other hand, my bestie and I were in the center part of the river where the water was going a little bit faster. And, actually, some areas were more than just a little bit faster which was quite fun.   As we were going down the river, we were holding onto each other's tubes as much as possible so as to stay together.   And so, there we were.....the current picking up pace, we were being swayed around rocks, spinning around at times, water splashing as the water moved a little faster and a little stronger. Quite a few other people were out on the water sitting in tubes enjoying themselves as well.

We noticed a family up ahead. They were holding onto each other's tubes creating a chain like a caterpillar of tubes weaving side to side as the river took them downstream.   Each their own tube....mom, dad, brothers, and sisters. Everyone was having fun. But, that was about to change in an instant.

A short section of the river was like a mini whitewater rapid with a couple of boulders toward the middle, breaking up the current. And there....up ahead, the tube chair caterpillar headed right into the whitewater which brought on squeals of excitement as the water gushed and splashed all around until the young girl who was in the last tube....was no longer in her tube.   The sheer power of the water from underneath pushed her out of her tube, propelled her in the air and she landed on a boulder, in the middle of the gushing river. It was a perfect landing as if an invisible hand simply plucked her off the tube and placed her gently onto the little boulder. One of those "you had to see it to believe it" moments and yet, there she was, sitting on that little boulder, water gushing all around.

The current was pretty strong in that section and we passed

her too quickly to grab her, but as we passed her, the look in her eyes was unmistakable. She sat there frozen with eyes open wide like round saucers. We could see the fear. While she didn't say it, the expression on her face and the look in her eyes said it loud and clear. "Help me!" The current had taken her family rapidly further downstream, and as we heard her father yelling out that "she can't swim", we also noticed in that split-second moment that she wasn't wearing a life vest.

This is where

the struggles you encounter introduce you to your strengths
- Epictetus, Greek philosopher

and this was a situation where a struggle introduced us to our strengths. We had the choice to follow the rules and to stay in our tubes. Just like in life, we had a choice to remain spectators or take control of our story. We had the choice of being bystanders or we could break the rules and jump into action, literally. As we passed right by her and saw the fear in her eyes, we knew which choice we needed to make. She was in so much fear that it was paralyzing her. It was one of those moments when my bestie and I looked at each other. We were both on the same wavelength. We knew that we had to jump in the water and help this little girl.

The water was not very deep. After all, with our feet on the slippery river bed, the water level was maybe up to the middle of our torso. Obviously, the water wasn't very deep in that section. It wasn't deep, but it was strong. We were fighting the current to make our way back to that little girl and it didn't dawn on me until later that, while this was taking place, a crowd of onlookers was gathering on the footbridge just above the river and they were watching to see what was happening. As they watched on, my bestie and I put our plan of action together rather quickly. She was going to make her way upstream to go above slightly past the little girl and then make her way back down. While she focused on that, I was coming upstream towards the little girl to be "the catcher" should there be a need.

We were so close. Oh my gosh..... my bestie had made her way upstream and was coming back down with her tube in hand. I was so close too. Almost within an arm's reach of the boulder where the little girl sat, motionless, watching as we got closer and closer from both sides. My bestie was just about to reach for the little girl and help her onto her swim tube when the current gushed again. It was such a big gush that it swept my bestie's feet right out from under her. She went feet first, downstream, passing the little girl. As she slipped downstream, she slipped straight into me which knocked my feet out from under and I went face down into the river.

It takes longer to tell the story than how fast it actually happened! It was all split-second moments. My bestie had quickly regained her footing and I could hear her screaming out my name "Marie-anne, Marie-anne" as she saw my tube, flipped over, twirling downstream and I was nowhere in sight. What she didn't know, is that thankfully, I had held onto the little handle of my tube as it flipped over and let the current take me downstream to a slower-moving area to get my footing back and that by having the tube flipped over, there was an air pocket and I had plenty of air to breathe. What an adventure!

We made our way back to that little girl. While it felt like forever, I would guesstimate that, from start to finish, it all happened in about ten minutes or less! We were able to help the little girl onto one of our tubes, got her reunited with her family that was waiting downstream after finding a place to pull off on the riverbank and we had an adventure we didn't expect that brought out our inner badasses!

After the happy family reunion, we got back into our tubes to complete our "tube the 'hooch" adventure. Yikes, during that whole escapade, my bestie bruised her tailbone from when her feet got swept out from under her and hit the river bottom, broke a toe, and was bleeding at the knees. I had some pretty nice bruises that appeared later on but here's something that was totally hilarious as our adventure came to an end. There was some red liquid running down my back that appeared to be coming from my scalp.

This is the funny part. Just before the trip, I had done a do-it-yourself hair dye job and I had dyed my hair, you guessed it, red! That was my first time ever dying my hair that color. Actually, I was pretty novice at hair dying and obviously hadn't rinsed it out completely. It's been years and I still crack myself up thinking of that visual, especially after such an adventure!

It was, for sure, a memorable comedy relief to break the seriousness of the whole, memorable, rule-breaking adventure.

Just like situations you may encounter in life, we did have a bit of a setback with how strong the current was and getting our feet swept out from under us. But that setback set us up for a nice comeback as we were determined to help that little girl.

We had the choice to let our concern consume us and have her wait for someone else to come along to help. We had a choice to let any fears take over and keep us from taking action. We had a choice to break the rules and take action. Yes, we did break the rules and took action. Sometimes people do not ask for help even when they need it. This little girl was the perfect example. She was so frozen in fear that she could not even ask for help.

Let me ask you a question.

Is asking for help out of your current comfort bubble? Is accepting help out of your current comfort bubble?

I invite you today to accept and ask for that support. I invite you today to step out of your current comfort bubble. Sometimes the secret sauce is letting go of that comfort bubble. Sometimes the secret sauce is asking for help. Sometimes the secret sauce is accepting help. Did you know that asking for help and accepting help will help you to break through barriers! Did you know that asking for help and accepting help is part of finding Your Inner Strength! Did you know that asking for help and accepting help makes you a badass!

4

⌒

Size doesn't matter

Size doesn't matter! I know that statements about size can be interpreted in a variety of ways. I even wrote an article years ago "When Bigger is Better" that got published in a B2B magazine. That article was about the pros and cons of business expansion.

Here I want to share with you about your own successes and that size doesn't matter because your journey is unique. Comparing doesn't work! I want you to celebrate all your successes, no matter the size. Now, there are two very important reasons as to why I want you to celebrate all your successes and you will discover why as we go along in this chapter. Let's start with the first one.

> *Even in the gloomiest of Valley the slightest glimmer of hope can spark a flame*
> Les Brown

I want you to think about that for a minute, "the slightest glimmer of hope can spark a flame." What may seem like a small success to one is going to be a giant success for another. What may seem like a small success to one is actually a slight glimmer of hope that can spark that flame again. So, I want you to remember that size is not what matters in the steps that you take and that the small successes no matter how small they may seem are steps that you can celebrate. And just like Walt Disney said, well he was one of the people credited with this quote....

It's not the extra mile but the extra inch that makes a difference.

That's so true when it comes to that extra inch. There have been so many times when I personally did not think I could go that extra inch. There have been so many times when I thought my rope was at its end. It was important for me to find those small wins to celebrate. But what do small wins even look like?

Well, let's think back at what was going on in my life that I shared in chapter one. That was a pretty intense time for me and once I found that glimmer of hope that sparked my flame, I needed to celebrate and recognize my wins, no matter the size. I needed to recognize each action that I was taking to take care of myself. The biggest win I had for weeks was drinking a single smoothie a day. I know. Some people might say, "oh big whoop! You drank a smoothie." But you know what, for me, it was huge that I was drinking a smoothie. Actually, drinking a smoothie a day was more food and good nutrition than what I had eaten in longer than I want to admit. You may remember that, at my lowest point, I was also my lowest weight of barely 90 pounds for a 5'2" body. So, once again, a smoothie a day may not be a big whoop for someone else, but it sure was a big whoop for me since that was the only food I was eating for the day.....and I was finally eating.

What else can a win look like? Maybe it is getting up in the morning when you don't feel like it. Maybe it is getting dressed instead of staying in pajamas all day long (now, I do collect onesie pajamas and have been known to stay in my onesie all day because I work from home and I love the comfort......yes, I have even been on zooms while wearing my onesies!). How about celebrating

Cooking a new dish

Making a couple of extra phone calls

Writing a letter of resignation....and turning it in

Paying off a credit card or a bill

Learning how to ride a bicycle

Getting a job or starting a business

Cleaning up the home

Learning to tie a necktie

Signing up for a class you've always wanted to take

Reading a book for personal development.....maybe it's this one!

Sewing a button onto a shirt

Maybe it is writing a book as "just" writing this book is a win for me. For some, writing a book is considered a small win. After all, they might have written many other books already. Why does it feel like a big win for me? Well, because it came from deciding not to muffle my voice anymore. It came from realizing that I did not need to "snuff my own light"

.....out of fear of what others may think,

.....out of fears of what others may say,

.....out of fears of how others may feel about me!

What may be a small win for you is a big win for somebody else and vice versa. And remember that size is not what matters. Just like Matilda said in the musical named *Matilda*

"even if you're little you can do a lot"

That is the same for your wins, your actions, and your steps. Even if they appear to be little, they can actually do a lot. Dismissing those wins is the same as snuffling your own voice. Learn from my experience. Learn from what I discovered the long way about. I want you to know and remember that snuffing your own light and your own voice does not serve anyone. It does not serve you and it does not serve others. It is actually doing the opposite. By snuffing out your light and muffling your voice, you are teaching others that they need to do the same. It is time to break that cycle. It is time to teach others that their light and their voice matter just as much as yours matters.

There is a huge difference between celebrating the wins and boasting or bragging and that is something I didn't grasp for the longest time. Have you ever been told not to share something because people would think you are bragging? Or maybe you might have noticed someone's sharing of a win and thought they were boasting? I have been guilty of this last one plenty of times.

First off, when celebrating wins, celebrating and sharing every detail of every single win may not always be the best idea. While I do not care what other people's opinions of me are anymore, meaning that their opinion doesn't change or dictate my thoughts and values, I also do not want to open the door to negative commentaries as there are some people in the world who make it their business to try and tear others down. Those people do exist, and I have no intention of inviting their words and energy into my life. Believe me, I did have that door open at one time and that negativity monster bit me in the tuchus......it bit hard!

I am now more mindful as to whom I share my wins with. I also remember to carve my successes and win in stone.....and any failures in the sand, keeping in mind that failures can still hold life lessons. Failures are the things that have gone wrong and I don't want to go with them! Failures are the things I do not want to repeat as I have learned lessons from those experiences. Failures are a beginning, not an end. Failures are not by accident, they have a purpose and we get to celebrate learning the lessons. Open your eyes to the possibilities and know that those are the wins to write in stone.

Celebrating daily is the consistency that keeps you going. Celebrating daily keeps the flame alive. Celebrating can also be that glimmer of hope should there be a moment or occasion that tries to snuff your flame. I even created a journal that has daily reminders to celebrate the wins.

Let's go back to that extra little inch that Walt Disney talks about. You know what? I want you to go ahead and stand up. Yes, stand up and put this book down. Have it open to this page on the table. You might need to have something to hold it open while you do this. Are you ready? This is going to be very simple. It's a cool little something I learned at one of the many conferences I have attended. I believe this is one from phenomenal keynote speaker, Brian Biro. If only my notes from back then were as organized as they are now, then I would be certain. But, on with this little exercise.

I want you to raise both of your arms in the air and raise your hands to the sky. Got them up? Good.

Next, while both your arms are raised, I want you to raise your left arm and reach higher just a little bit more. An extra inch or so will do.

Did you do it? I bet you did. That's perfect. Now you can relax your arms, and sit back down to keep on reading. You may be wondering. Why did I have you stand up and do that? No, it wasn't to get the blood circulating, although that is a good idea. Let's examine this a little.

When I first asked you to put your arms up in the air and raise your hands to the sky, you did it and it was only natural that you did not reach as high as possible. It was only natural that you had the ability to go a little bit more and you might even have been able to reach more than an extra inch. It is the same in life. We all have the ability to do a little bit more and that little bit more is another win for you to celebrate. Those little wins can be life-changing.

I have one more story to share about small things! Sometimes that little bit more is the one thing that makes a world of a difference. I learned the weirdest thing about lobsters. Well, I think it's weird but then, I am not a lobster and if you know lobsters, let me know if you have noticed this phenomenon as I haven't been able to find more info on this. I learned that a lobster will stay put on a rock while waiting for the waves to come and get it instead of moving just a little to get into the nearby water. It waits. I learned that the lobster, by not moving, will die. If the lobster was to move just a little bit to reach the water, that would be a small win with life-changing results wouldn't you say?

Before we go onto the next chapter together, I need for you to stop and recognize wins you have personally experienced yourself within the last week. It doesn't matter how small they may appear, I want you to recognize and celebrate them. Go ahead. Write them down. I am even making space for you right here.

1

2

3

4

5

6

7

8

The smallest wins can be the most life changing.

5

✺

You hold the Power

Why did the chicken cross the road? To get to the other side.

I am guessing that you probably heard that joke before. Where I live, it feels like there are chickens everywhere. I was even on a call while sitting in the parking lot at the grocery store and the person on the other end asked what the noise in the background was. My unphased answer was a simple "Oh, that's just a chicken" which brought on an amused giggle from the other person who lives in a city, and wild chickens that are so tame to hang around parking lots were not something she was expecting to hear.

I want you to pay close attention the next time you see a chicken crossing the road while you are driving. I want you to pay close attention to what the chicken does and more specifically, what the chicken doesn't do. As you drive closer and closer, the majority of the time, what you will witness is the chicken will go back where it came from instead of finishing to cross the street.

Unless the chicken knows what is on the other side of the road, it will choose to go back to what it knows. The comfort bubble is where it was. The comfort bubble is what it knows. The comfort bubble is not on the other side of the road!

One thing that we know for sure is that

> ### *The only thing constant is change.*
> Heraclitus

Crossing the road to get to the other side is a change. For a chicken, that is a big change! How you handle change and what you do about it are actions that are within your power. Yes, you hold the power and you have the power to decide the direction of your future. You hold the power with your habits. You hold the power with your words. You hold the power with what you stand for. I love the line in the song co-written by Aaron Tippin and Buddy Brock

> ### *You've got to stand for something or you'll fall for anything*

Yes.....I am singing that line instead of simply reading it. Did you sing too?

One thing you need to stand for is your own personal development. Abram Maslow, a psychologist that passed away before I was even born, points out that

> ### *If the only tool you have is a hammer,*
> ### *it is tempting to treat everything as if it were a nail*

Personal development expands the tools we have in the tool-box of our minds. Instead of just hammers, we add wrenches, screwdrivers, hacksaws, and whatever other tools we may need. And, Albert Einstein put it eloquently when he said that we cannot solve our problems with the same thinking we used when we created them. Whether we are looking to fix problems or change situations and circumstances, it is imperative to change our thinking and equip our minds with a variety of tools. By changing our thinking, we then change our actions and by changing our actions, we change outcomes. Personal development influences our thinking, our words, our feelings, and our actions. If all you take away and apply from this book is the information from this chapter, your life as you know it will be completely different in the near future. No. I am not saying to only read this chapter, what I am saying is that this chapter is roughly in the middle of the book because the topic needs to be at the center of everything you do. Personal development is at the core of it all.

Looking back on history, many individuals already understood the power of the mind, our thoughts, our words, our feelings, and our actions. Benjamin Franklin, back in the 1700s, is one great example. I highly recommend that you read about his life and his involvement in the creation of the library system. Another great example is Carter Godwin Woodson who is known as the "Father of Black History". It is so true what Mr. Woodson says about what man thinks. He believed that if you can determine what someone thinks, you will be able to determine how they will act. He goes on to explain that if you control what someone thinks of themselves, you will control the path of their actions. If you have control over someone and make them feel inferior or an outcast, they will in turn behave so.

The mind, our thoughts, and our words, are very powerful. Having that awareness comes with great responsibility to ourselves and others.

So let us go ahead and talk about investing in yourself. Don't just take my word for it. Whether I am quoting Warren Buffett's

The most important investment you can make is in yourself.

Or one of my mentors, Les Brown, a powerful motivational speaker, author, and former radio DJ among many other hats, is adamant about the importance of investing "at least 10% of your income into personal development because it is much more expensive to be ignorant than it is to invest in learning. The road to personal development never ends." I do have to agree. During the year 2020, I invested more than 10% of my income into personal development, including learning directly from Mr. Les Brown, and believe me when I say that there is never a dull moment when he is in the room, even virtually.

Everything keeps on changing around the world. You might have noticed or experienced the transition in the workforce that if one doesn't grow, learn, and expand.....one is expandable and replaceable.

Even Alvin Toffler, predicted back in 1970 in his book *Future Shock* that "the illiterate of the twenty-first century will not be those who cannot read and write, but those who cannot learn, unlearn and relearn." Wow! That is so true. So many things that I had learned over the years were the very things I needed to unlearn. I learned lessons from people in my life who didn't know any better and yet their advice, their words, and their guidance was the very same that I needed to unlearn which is why I worked harder on myself than anything else during the covid shutdown. Don't get me wrong. I worked in a psychiatrist's office and applied myself to my job. I would not have served the patients, my employer, or myself if I didn't do my best. And with that said, it was important for me to work on myself to let my light shine the way it was and is meant to shine. In order to do that, I knew that I needed to find the right mentors and coaches.

For years, I had been using the wrong tools! It's like Jack's Mother said to Jack in *"Into The Woods"*

A slotted spoon holds little soup

If I want to release the powerful voice that has been muffled within me for so many years, then I need to learn from someone that has a powerful voice. And that is exactly what I did with Les Brown. That single decision was the catalyst to changing the focus of this book, otherwise, you would be reading all about my training sessions, thoughts while out for our runs, and much more. That single decision was also the catalyst to me hiring a business coach when I transitioned from the W-2 world combined with being a serial entrepreneur to being an energetic speaker, author, Gratitude Coach, and serial entrepreneur all in one big swoop.

What do you want to do in your life? What do you need to learn? Success leaves clues so who do you need to be learning from? Maybe you don't know yet what you need to unlearn or learn. After all, I didn't know what I didn't know and I am willing to bet that it is the same for you. And if you don't even know which direction you need to take yet, start by learning something new and tackling it with a sense of adventure. If you realize along the way that what you are tackling is not aligning with you, then you are on the path to discovering what is.

You hold the power and the key to your future. As you learn and tackle something new with a sense of adventure, I am going to recommend four key daily habits and focus to adopt, if you do not already do so.

The first one is about the energy you give to your day. We are going to look at making a small change to your morning routine if you aren't already doing something like this. This may mean getting up an extra 30 minutes early to have some quiet time for it, especially so that you can still do the rest of your traditional morning routines such as getting kids ready for their day or anything else you might normally be doing when you first get up.

What you do at the very start of your day, sets the tone for your day. I didn't realize how important this step actually is until I got my groove of doing it daily. Getting up 30 minutes earlier while I was working at the psychiatrist meant getting way earlier than I wanted to, but it was crucial for me to do so and now that I am no longer punching someone else's clock, I do have the liberty to sleep more and that feels so good.

The morning consists of first and foremost feeding the cat as she is queen and if her human is up, that can only mean that she is being tended to hand and foot! Once her highness is cared for, then it is onto my routine. I have a drink I make myself every morning, and have been doing it for years. Apple cider vinegar, lemon juice, and cayenne pepper are three of the six ingredients. I call it my gogo juice as I don't need coffee to get me going. Once my drink is ready, I take my time to enjoy it while I write in my daily log book.

1. I am Thankful and Grateful for .....
2. Today's #1 goal is.....
3. Today's To-Do list is....
4. My why.....
5. My #1 yearly goal is....
6. My #1 monthly goal is.....
7. My #1 quarterly goal is.....
8. Daily disciplines to check off and make sure I do them, including taking my supplements, reading and/or listening to audios, journaling my I AM statements, water intake, and even sending cards as I am an avid card sender.

And at the end of the day, I pull out my daily log to add

1. A win for the day to celebrate
2. Any notes on something to improve
3. Who did I share my gratitude and appreciation with
4. Something that I learned

Now you may be wondering why some of those are written down daily in my logbooks, such as the goals and my why, especially since I also have pages dedicated to writing out and planning the goals and so on. It is very simple. It is because of how the brain functions. The brain is amazing and even more specifically, the subconscious part of the brain! What I have noticed from my own practice of this step is that my daily actions are more likely to align with what I need to do to reach those goals when I write them down daily. If you don't believe me, take the next two months to experiment. Do an entire month without these steps and then an entire month with these steps. Note the difference in your own actions....or better yet, learn from my own experience and save yourself valuable time! You hold the power and this is a powerful way to harness that power.

Habit and focus #2 is what this entire chapter has been focusing on.....personal development. In this particular case, personal development through reading. There is tremendous power in the words you read. There is tremendous power in the words that you listen to. There is tremendous power in the words that you use. This could easily become an entire chapter but in a nutshell, be mindful of what you watch on the television, listen to on the radio, or read on the internet/newspaper/books. Make the conscious choice to read on a daily basis on topics that are uplifting and will help you in becoming the person you were born to be. Believe me when I say this took me a while. I would start reading and my eyes would get all drowsy until I found that the best time for me to read was in the morning as part of my daily routine after journaling. And I know that this may sound weird, but I prop up whichever book I am reading on top of the washing machine and walk in place while reading aloud. This works great for me and I can do it without waking anyone else up. What kind of books do I read? I read books by a variety of authors ranging from Les

Brown to Ivan Misner to Rachel Hollis. Be sure to check the addendum for a list of books I suggest.

Habit and focus #3 is to share your gratitude and appreciation with someone each day. While this is a topic of huge interest as a Gratitude Coach, and I could write a book on this topic, I will keep it brief. Well, actually, I will be writing a book on this topic so stay tuned! When it comes to gratitude and appreciation, I like to do this as part of my daily morning routine when I write "I am Thankful and Grateful for...." and list names of people who are making a positive impact in my life. From that list, I then send a note of appreciation in the mail to one of those individuals. You see, doing so releases dopamine in my brain. Dopamine is a naturally occurring chemical in the brain that creates feelings of pleasure. What an awesome way to start my day! Not only am I sending a note that brings joy to someone else, but it also starts my day off with pleasure. It is a natural high and one of the only things I would suggest getting addicted to. It's a win-win habit. I like to sprinkle joy and gratitude around like glitter and if you have ever worked with glitter, you know that when you sprinkle it around, some is bound to stick to you. Another reason why it is key to write words of gratitude for others is that it is technically impossible for the brain to have a negative thought simultaneously. It is impossible for positive and negative thoughts to exist at the exact same time. This is a powerful habit with many more benefits. And like I said, it is a topic in an upcoming book.

Habit and focus #4 is with the words you choose to say to yourself and to others. There are enough negative words used all around us to last us multiple lifetimes. Are you aware that it takes hearing positive words an average of 17 times to negate hearing a single negative word? Negative words can be said with the best intentions in mind. For example, a school counselor might tell a student that the student cannot draw so being an artist would not be a good career and they need to look at another vocation. From my own experience, I have been told that I could not sing and didn't belong in the choir.....and then the teacher pointed me to the door. This was back in elementary school and I do mean it literally, the teacher said to me "you can't sing." Do you know how many years it took for me to even get the courage to get on stage and do something that I love, even after being told that I couldn't do it? I was an adult with 3 children when I finally worked up the courage to do what I had wanted to do as a child. And yes, I now sing to my heart's content. While my singing may not meet some people's standards, I can sing and I have enjoyed singing on stage at our local theater where my first singing line was singing three little words "Praise to Buddha" as a royal wife in The King and I. Now that you know the impact of words, choose words wisely.

To recap, the habit and focus are

#1 set the energy you give to your day with your daily routine of how you start and the energy with how you end your day

#2 personal development with your reading and/or listening

#3 share your gratitude and appreciation with someone each day

#4 be aware of the words you say to yourself and others

These simple habits and focus are catalysts to releasing your inner badass. They will show you that you have the power within you to break through barriers that were built from accepting other people's words about you and very importantly, that you are stronger than you realize!

6

꩜

Your Genius is in the Empty Spaces

Your Genius is in the Empty Spaces. What do you think I mean by that?

Have you ever experienced being on a long, monotonous drive, and all of a sudden you start to get ideas and solutions to problems that were on your mind previously? Or maybe you noticed this happens to you when you are taking a nice, long, relaxing shower or a long, hot, relaxing bubble bath, which if you have little ones can be very rare and long in between. Or how about, when you are in bed and the flow of ideas is keeping you awake!

If you are like me, you probably have pens and pads of paper in places like your car, your purse or bag, next to your bed, your desk, and possibly even more places. You too may be using voice recording apps or sending yourself emails from your phone to make sure you remember the genius thoughts that come to you.

Why does this happen? Let's get a little nerdy without going super deep.

Your brain activity creates currents that can be measured in hertz. At this point, it looks like scientists have identified 5 different types of brainwaves and I wonder if there are even more. They are called Delta, Theta, Alpha, Beta, and Gamma waves. While each wave pattern has its benefits, you get to tap into your genius, and creativity when you are both awake and relaxed, and when you have increased alpha wave activity. This can be right when you wake up in the morning. This can be just before you go to sleep and personally, this has kept me up for hours at times so having a notepad handy is helpful. This can be while getting a massage (good luck writing notes then) or while meditating. Scientists are also saying that exercise can create the brain to have an increase in alpha wave activity and based on my experiences while marathon training, I would care to agree. And while it has been noted that alpha waves boost creativity by an average of 7.4%, I do wonder how the scientists in the Cortex journal, a journal devoted to the study of the nervous system and behavior, are able to be so precise in their measurement of creativity.

But what are some ways you can increase the Alpha wave activity? It can be achieved in a variety of ways so I encourage you to explore and discover which one is best suited to you. You may have heard already that the blue light emitted from electronics and some light sources affect the quality of sleep as well as create brain stress. A very simple remedy would be to check the blue light settings of your electronic devices like cell phones and computers.

There are also blue-light-blocking glasses available from a variety of places. I have a reading glass prescription and I was pleasantly surprised to find a store online offering a set of blue-light-blocking reading glasses in the strength that I need which is perfect for having one in the car, one in my bag, one at my desk, and so on. Of course, your ophthalmologist can help you if you wear glasses in order to see clearly!

It's funny how sometimes you can be doing something naturally and then, later on, learn what that actually does. Music is one of them. There are certain types of music and sounds that I noticed help me in staying focused while the creativity is flowing. Binaural beats! Always learning something new and loving it. Apparently, the choices of music and sounds that I have been making have binaural beats incorporated. In a way, it is like the brain uses the binaural beats as a tuning fork and to tune into the alpha state. It is amazing how instinctively, we can be drawn to exactly what we need. If you are curious as to what those sound like, you can do a search online. There are many to be found that range from 45 minutes in length up to over 9 hours. I personally have a 9+ hour soundtrack bookmarked for speedy online access.

Now here's one that you may already be doing! Let's talk about meditation. Did you know that the sense of peacefulness, calm and focus you experience during meditation is brought on by an increase in alpha waves? Studies have been conducted with Zen monks and the overall conclusion is that they have extraordinary synchronicity of their brain waves when meditating. Pretty cool. I have heard meditation being referred to as the old-school version of neurofeedback which we will look into as well in just a moment. If meditation is something you already practice on a regular basis, and when I say regular, I mean even 5 minutes daily, that is fantastic. If meditation is something you would like to explore, there are a plethora of offline and online resources available ranging from free apps, to recorded videos, to meditation guides and more. The funny thing I have noticed when I meditate is the sensation of floating......literally feeling like I am not touching the ground. It's a pretty cool sensation that dissipates as soon as the eyelids crack open. If meditation is your thing, I would suggest venturing to test out some yoga routines as well as that very well may be your Genius space. Explore around and discover.

Neurofeedback is something I have explored a little bit with a session so that I could have first-hand experience of it. The session started off by sitting in a comfortable reclined chair and having little electrodes set on different areas of the head to get a measurement of the before-neurofeedback brainwave activity. Once that was recorded, with the electrodes remaining in place, I simply got to listen to sounds while watching a monitor. It was very calming and soothing sitting there, in the reclining chair, looking at the images changing on the screen in front of me while listening to those sounds, which now, thinking back, were probably binaural beats. The images were more like squiggles slowly moving and morphing rather than actual pictures. At the end of the session, another reading of the brainwave activity was taken to do a comparison of the before and after. I have to say, I was surprised to experience something so simple and yet so impactful. The gal that I went to for the session uses neurofeedback to successfully help those who have experienced a traumatic brain injury and those with diagnoses such as attention deficit disorder, anxiety, and hyperactivity to name just a few in both adults and children. If you would like to experience neurofeedback, it is important to work with someone who is properly trained as there is a science to it.

My understanding is that some people are able to use either neurofeedback, meditation, or binaural beats to train their brains to switch on and keep on, the alpha waves which is phenomenal. Being able to create that empty space, boost the alpha waves, and release your genius is powerful and I have one more possible way for you to do that. Being a Gratitude Coach, I saved this part for last.

The double-sided coin of forgiveness and gratitude is more powerful than most even imagine especially when done together as one. We are going to do this together right now. Let me preface this by letting you know right now that this exercise may be the hardest section of the book for you to complete and I want you to be ready to take some time afterward for some self-care such as by taking a long shower, going for a walk, or maybe even taking a cat-nap. This is an exercise that can help you unload emotions hiding and creating stress from past experiences or trauma. This process will help you to let it go, and find gratitude through and within the forgiveness. When I did it myself, I pretty much went to bed afterward and slept like a baby.

Let's walk through the 5 step process together once and you can repeat it afterward as many times as you feel the need to.

Step 1. Write about a situation, moment, or person that hurt or wronged you. Sometimes, that person is even ourselves. For the moment, simply pick one occasion or person to do this exercise about. I'm leaving some space right here for you to do that right now:

Step 2. Next, it is time to dig a little into it. I know how hard that can get. I was in tears doing this part and believe me when I say that it does help. Be open and honest with yourself. Hiding it down deep only keeps you from achieving your greatness and from releasing your inner badass. I have witnessed this over and over again. So, go ahead and write down how it made you feel. Let it all out. No holds barred.

Step 3. Now it is time to acknowledge those feelings. Just for a few minutes. Close your eyes, feel the emotions, and let the tears run down your cheeks if that is the space you are in at the moment. As you close your eyes, remember that this is just for a few minutes because it is important to acknowledge in order to be able to move forward.

Step 4. Now that you have acknowledged those feelings, you also verbalized them by writing them down, it is time for you to actually feel gratitude. Feel gratitude because somehow that particular situation, that particular moment, or that particular person has shaped you into the amazing, stellar, badass you are today. Yes, even if the badass within you hasn't fully emerged yet, I know it is getting ready to reveal itself. You got this book and are doing the work because you know it is your time to reveal your inner badass. So go ahead. Look at those experiences from the past and see that there was a gift hiding within. As you look for the gift, I want you to discover that YOU are the gift. YOU are the treasure. As you realize you are the gift that was hiding in those experiences, feel the gratitude for what you have been through and move on to the last step.

Step 5. Forgive! Forgive what happened in that particular situation, that particular moment, or that particular person that hurt or wronged you. Making the conscious decision to forgive after feeling gratitude is such a huge leap in moving forward with who you are meant to be as it lifts the weight of emotions and mental stress. I want you to remember that forgiving is not saying that what has taken place in the past was okay. It simply means that you are ready to let go and move on. You have no more need to hold it and bury it all down deep. You probably have heard the analogy about holding onto those emotions is like holding a hot stone and you are the only one getting burned. Go ahead. Stop the burning. Let go of that hot stone. Forgive.

As I said, this is probably the hardest of the action steps in this book and there can be deeper work that can be done with this as well. I personally defer that part to my own coach as that is part of her genius. Now that you have completed this process once, you will want to go through this exercise and repeat it for other situations, moments, or people who have hurt you. Remember to allow yourself the time and space to recharge yourself afterward. Give yourself permission to take that catnap, go for that walk, take that bubble bath, or even get that massage!

I want to celebrate with you this big step you just took. Letting go of emotions that have been holding you down, that have been holding you back from becoming who you are meant to be. Pause for a moment, stand up, take a deep breath, and claim this out loud. Say it out loud....

I matter.

My voice matters.

Experiences from the past had a gift within.

I looked for the gift and discovered that I AM the gift.

I AM a treasure.

I AM BadAss.

One more time....with more oomph, more gusto!

I matter.
My voice matters.
Experiences from the past had a gift within.
I looked for the gift and discovered that I AM the gift.
I AM a treasure.
I AM BadAss.

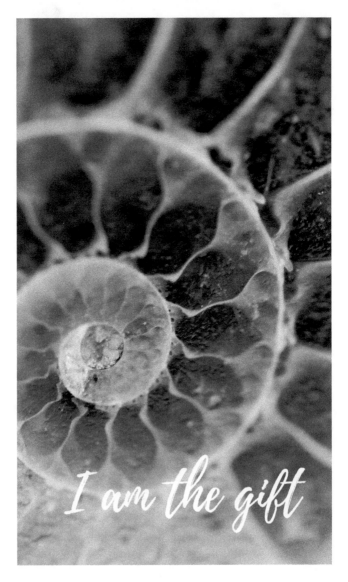

I am the gift

7

❧

Let Your Light Shine

Over the years, I have realized that there are two main reasons why some people are not letting their light shine. One is as a way to people-please: what we think is how we are supposed to be. The other is by not asking or accepting help. Do either one or maybe both, ring true for you?

Let us start with the latter as that is something I was doing. I was trying to honor someone I love being just like her and not realizing that it was holding me back from embracing my greatness! It was holding me back from letting my light shine to its bright potential. It was even hiding it away at times. Maybe that is something you can relate to. Maybe you are doing it right now. Maybe you used to do this and have already made the realization that asking for support is a much better way to honor that person. I love my mom so much that I was being..... just like her. My mom was always doing things for others but never doing things for herself. My mom was always putting everyone else first. My mom was always doing everything without asking for help and I did not realize that I was following in her footsteps.

Subconsciously, I was always doing things for others but never for myself.....in order to honor my mom.
Subconsciously, I was putting everyone else first......in order to honor my mom.

Subconsciously, I was trying to do everything without asking for help......in order to honor my mom.

But then.....I had an Aha! Moment and needed to change "the recording" in my subconscious that manifested in those actions. Instead, I get to greatly honor my mom by changing the pattern, changing "the recording" and changing the paradigm.

Consciously, I now do things for myself as well as for others.....in order to honor my mom and myself.

Consciously, I now put myself first .....in order to honor my mom and myself, which as you will read later on is not a selfish thing to do like I used to think! I am making progress to change this paradigm and I do revert to my old patterns. With more awareness, I am now making the conscious shift. The more I do it, the easier it gets to shift and the same is for you.
Consciously, I now ask for help.....in order to honor my mom and myself. This one too has some back and forth going on of "trying" to do it all myself and asking for help from others. I know the day will come when asking for help for me comes naturally, to the same degree as asking for help for others comes naturally already.

I am sure that you already know all this and yet knowing is different from applying. There are times when a reminder is needed. This is your reminder should you be in need of it. Help is a two-way street. There are those that need help and there are those that give the help. If you are like me, helping others is definitely not a challenge. If you are like me, the challenge is to accept help.... not accepting because of not asking for it and also not accepting it when offered. Would it help you to ask for and accept support if you knew that by doing so, you are giving someone else a chance to shine? I want this to really sink in. Opening yourself to receiving from others gives them a chance to shine their light. It gives them a chance to shine their light just the same as yours shines when you do the giving. When I had that realization, it hit me like "WoW!" This is huge! Trying to do it all myself not only isn't serving me, and isn't effective, but it also robs others from being able to shine their light.

Is this an epiphany moment for you?

This is huge! Think about it...... What kind of world can we live in by allowing everyone to shine their light!

I know in my heart, in every fiber of my being, that I never intended to rob anyone of the opportunity to shine their light, and yet that is what I have been doing for so many years. With each new day, there is a new opportunity to shine your light and invite others to shine theirs!

Let's illustrate what that can look like. On average, an American football stadium has the capacity to seat 69,444 people and you are 1 among 69,443 others. You are standing in the very first row, the one closest to the field. We are going to imagine two examples together.

The first example is trying to do it all yourself. Imagine that it is dark and every single person in the stadium is standing, holding a candle that needs to be lit, including yours.....and you happen to have a lighter! You don't ask for help, maybe it is simply because you don't want to impose on anyone. You go to each person and light their candle, one by one. Your thumb starts to feel the heat from the lighter and the more candles you light, the hotter it gets until you get burned but you keep going. You are making some headway, after all, you have lit every single candle on the first row. Some offer to help which you politely decline. Now you start lighting the candles for people in the second row, but your lighter fluid runs out! You resort to using your own candle to light the others. It doesn't make your light any lesser but all the effort and time is causing your wax to melt and burn. Your flame dies before you can even finish lighting the candles in the second row.

For the second example, you are in the same American football stadium where you are 1 of the 69,444 people. Once again, you are standing in the very first row closest to the field. And once again, every single person has a candle that needs to be lit and yes, you do happen to have a lighter. You light your candle and put away the lighter. You turn to your right and using your flame, you light the candle of that person. Then you turn to your left and using your flame, you light the candle of that person. And lastly, you turn to the person behind you and using your flame, you light their candle. This is where the magic happens. You ask those three people to help and light the candles of those around them like you just did and to ask them to light the candles of those around them. As they each do the same, more and more candles are lit and before you know it, every single candle in the stadium is lit while yours is still shining bright.

In the first scenario, not only did you do a disservice to yourself by trying to do it all yourself and not allowing others to help even when they offered, but you also lost the ability to keep your own light shining before everyone's candle got lit with the majority of the people still standing in the dark. In the second scenario, not only do you still have fluid in your lighter, but your light still shining bright and by asking for help, you have made it possible for 69,443 others to have their light shine and the entire stadium is glowing so brightly that the light can be seen from miles around.

If you are trying to do it all yourself to the detriment of your own light, remember that the world is a much better place when you allow others to support and shine their light alongside yours. Invite and allow others to shine their light so you too can have your light shine.

As I shared earlier, there are two main reasons why some people are not letting their light shine. One is as a way to people-please: what we think is how we are supposed to be. The other is by not asking or accepting help and we have already talked about the latter. Not letting your light shine as a way to fit in or people-please can be stemming from a variety of reasons. Most commonly, from my own experience of people-pleasing and from what I have observed in others and my coaching clients, it is out of wanting to fit in, wanting to avoid conflict, feeling guilty when saying "no" to others and needing to be validated by others. Keep in mind these are the most common and not, by any means, an exhaustive or comprehensive list.

As a people-pleaser, I was saying "yes" to almost everything! You need help with a fundraiser....of course, I can help. You need a ride.....I sure can rearrange my schedule for you. You call me on the phone because you need to vent, moan and groan......that's okay, I can put everything else on hold. I would feel so bad if I said "no" and, of course, would have to go into the "why I can't" explanation hoping that the other person would not be upset about it. "I'm sorry" was frequently uttered even when there was no need for me to apologize. It is a vicious cycle. It is a stressful cycle and I was putting way too much pressure on myself to the point that my light wasn't shining as it should. It's the kind of stuff that can lead to health-related issues both physical and mental, such as anxiety and depression.

I am going to share with you some tips that have helped me and my clients.

- Give yourself with the same grace and understanding that you give to others.
- When others say that they can't do something, you don't expect them to give you an explanation and know they don't need you to explain yourself either. I have learned to say that I have a prior commitment and, yes, sometimes that prior commitment is time set aside for myself.
- When someone shares with you that they are making time for self-care and you are happy for them, remember to do the same for yourself!
- Give yourself time to evaluate if you can or really want to do something.....determine which is best for you.
- Ask yourself if what is being asked of you aligns with your values, your goals, and your vision.
- By being yourself and letting your light shine, you will attract to you the people who appreciate you for who you are and there won't be the desire to "try" to fit in by being someone you aren't!

You cannot truly serve others or live your purpose by dimming your light in any way. Bring honor to yourself and to those you love by letting your light shine.

Share your true voice......*it needs to be heard.*
Shine your true light......*it needs to be seen.*

Share your true voice......
            it needs to be heard.
Shine your true light......
            it needs to be seen.

8

◈

A daily slice of PIE

After reading this last chapter, you will never look at a slice of pie the same again! Yes, I want you to have a daily slice of PIE. What a wonderful coincidence, or is it a coincidence, that as I am writing this last chapter, my husband and I ran into Salty, a friend, who shared a vision of his that involves a plethora of pies!

While I am already salivating at the thought of a good, home-made, apple, peach, or cherry pie....mmmmmmmm, that isn't the type of pie I am talking about for now. But if you want to enjoy a yummy slice while you read on, go right ahead and enjoy. Sounds like a pretty darn good idea to me.

Let's get down to our topic. I want you to think of PIE as an acronym, or better yet, a recipe for daily living.

P = Passion & Purpose
I = Intensity & Intention
E = Embrace a Mindset of Abundance

Over the years, I have interviewed and met individuals who have completely changed around their focus in life. Many of them actually became entrepreneurs because of the P part of PIE! Passion and Purpose! Now I do want you to understand that being an entrepreneur as part of the "P", is for some but not for all. Some people know very early on what lights their fire, fans their flame, and what impact they were born to have in this world. Others, me included, take a little while longer and have to experience a variety of challenges to help us discover, or uncover, the gift we have within. The journey of self-discovery is filled with adventures. And yes, you probably already know that not all adventures are easy, breezy, and smooth sailing. Those experiences are part of the process to instill in us a strong belief, deep down into every fiber of our being, of what we are here for. It is through those experiences that we become unshakeable in who we are. It is through those experiences that we release our inner badass.

Our Passion and Purpose may have nothing to do with what we do for income. When we do what we are passionate about, and live our purpose, there is an inner peace we get to experience. There is a sense of joy that cannot be attained from materialistic acquisitions. There is a sense of knowing that you are where you are meant to be, doing what you are meant to do, and being the person you were born to be. Your purpose is part of a bigger picture, a masterpiece, with each piece crucial in creating the whole......each creating an impact. The size of the impact is not what matters. The impact is what matters. The impact is what you are here for. As you discover and live your "P", I want you to think of the impact you create as being a very crucial piece in the masterpiece of life.

For some, the "P" is manifested in what may seem to be small moments or small actions in the grandeur of life, but do not be mistaken by size as one small pebble can create a rippling effect that crosses an entire lake. The "P" can manifest in simple acts of kindness. You may have heard stories of individuals whose lives have been changed simply by a stranger's random act of kindness. Well, they may seem to be random acts of kindness, but what I have observed over the years is that they occur when one is in tune, or in alignment, you could say, with one's purpose. Those "random" acts of kindness turn out to be exactly what is needed in those specific moments. There are individuals who are born to be a ray of hope in the lives of others, even if just for a brief moment before moving on to what awaits them next, or while they wait for the next individual they are meant to shine a light for. They are like sporadic drops of sunshine and they are not born to shine in other people's lives on a constant basis.

And then there are others whose "P" is more apparent on a daily basis and as they discover that their "P" is, they are the ones who are drawn to more specific professions or ways to be a contributor in this world. A great example of that is one of the guests on my Red Gloves Chat show. She left a very well-paying position, with benefits, to become an entrepreneur. She was great at her job in the world of IT and enjoyed what she did. Over time, she discovered that her passion is to help the kupunas. Kupuna is a word you hear often if you live in Hawaii. It is used to refer with respect for elders and grandparents. As my guest discovered that her "P" was not in the world of IT, she took action steps to shift and pivot in order to live her "P"! That is now what she does full-time and her heart's cup is full.

Maybe your purpose is to be a positive glimpse of light in the lives of others just for a brief moment so they each can have hope again. Maybe your passion and purpose is something that is meant for you to be doing as a profession, whether it is for yourself or working for someone else. Maybe it is something you do from a philanthropic point of view. Whether or not you know what your "P" is at this very moment, remember that the journey to discovering it is part of the process that doesn't have a specific timeline which brings me to the "I" of PIE.

The "I" is for intensity and intention. If you look at the definition of these words, intensity can be described as an extreme state of strength, force, energy, or feeling. Intention, when it comes to how we live, has to do with living with meaning and purpose instead of being on autopilot or mindless with our thoughts and actions.

What I am inviting you to do is to put a certain level of energy and feeling into the actions you do on a daily basis. I am inviting you to make the conscious choice of how you want to live your life and the impact you are creating with those choices. What is the outcome you would like to see? Will your choice create an outcome that feels right, or is in alignment, with your "P"? Will your choice bring you closer to living your 'P'?

I don't know all the details of what is going on in your life and some of this may feel overwhelming just reading about it, especially when you feel drawn to live with "P" and "I" while having a full plate of things you need to deal with. Some people find it very easy to write up a list each day of 5 things they will do that day to get them closer to being able to live their "P" and "I". For others, having 1 thing, 1 task, and 1 step, no matter what size it is, is the best that can be done at the moment. By aligning yourself daily to your passion and purpose, setting the intentions and intensity, you will create a shift in your life that will help you to live your "P" and "I" effortlessly and mindfully. Remember. It is not the size that matters.

Both the "P" and "I" are important components in the recipe of life......so is the "E" if you want PIE! The "E" in PIE is for embracing a mindset of abundance. I do realize that there is an appearance of limitations based on many examples all around us. And yet, there are even bigger examples of abundance if we are open to witnessing them. There is an abundance of resources. There is an abundance of ideas. There is an abundance of kindness. There is an abundance of collaboration. There is an abundance of talent. There is an abundance of stars. These are just a few examples! The more you practice the daily habits outlined in chapter 5, the more examples of abundance you will notice and experience.

Now that you know what PIE stands for, let your Badass self apply daily the steps we covered together in the chapters of this book and have a daily slice of PIE!

YOU have what it takes to break through your barriers!
YOU have the ability to tap into your inner strength!
YOU truly are a Badass!

BONUS SECTION

I invite you to go on a 30-day journey of personal development, discovery, and transformation. Each day's activity has space for you to do your writing. Day 1 and Day 2 are focusing on developing your I AM statements. The rest of the days, you will be doing 2-minute Journaling. You will set a timer for 2 minutes and journal based on the question or prompt provided for that day.

SCAN ME

Day 1

Today is focusing on setting a strong foundation of I AM statements and affirmations. Plan on about 10 minutes each day with the exception of today which is foundational. Go to this link to watch the video https://youtu.be/Hkk8eNLV1io (or scan the QR code).

Use the next pages for notes

Day 2

Today I want you to focus on the I AM statements and affirmations you worked on yesterday. Read them out loud to yourself. Make any changes you want to make. Add any that you want to add. This may sound like a very simple activity, however, there is great power in your words. You will be reading your list daily. Starting tomorrow, there will be a second step to your daily activity. Use this page and the next to rewrite all your statements so you can have them nicely organized together.

Day 3

Step 1 - Read your I AM statements and affirmations out loud to yourself.

Step 2 - Your 2-minute journaling question/prompt: **What have you accomplished in the last year that you're proud of?**

Day 4

Step 1 - Read your I AM statements out loud for yourself.

Step 2 - Set a timer for 2 minutes and journal on this: **If you were gifted 10K to spend in 24 hours, what would you do with it? It is for spending, not investing. What is 1 thing you would spend it on? Expand and write on those details.**

Day 5

Step 1 - Read out loud to yourself your I AM statements & affirmations. If you want to look at yourself in the mirror while you do this and... it is important that you always, always, always, do the reading before going on to step 2.

Step 2 - 2 Minute Journaling about: **If you could teleport to 1 place and stay there for 24 hours, where would you go and what would you do?**

Day 6

Step 1 - Read out loud to yourself your I AM statements & affirmations. It is important that you always, always, always, do the reading before going on to step 2.

Step 2 - 2 Minute Journaling. Set your timer for 2 minutes and journal about **a challenge you have experienced that has made you stronger.**

Day 7

Step 1 - Read out loud to yourself your I AM statements & affirmations.

Step 2 - 2 Minute Journaling: **What would your closest friends and family say is your best quality?**

Day 8

Step 1 - Step 1 - Read out loud to yourself your I AM statements & affirmations.

Step 2 - 2 Minute Journaling: **Something you experienced in the past that you are still healing from and need to remind yourself to give yourself grace.**

Day 9

Step 1 - Step 1 - Read out loud to yourself your I AM statements & affirmations.

Step 2 - 2 Minute Journaling: **What are three simple things you can do each day to love on yourself?**

Day 10

Step 1 - Step 1 - Read out loud to yourself your I AM statements & affirmations.

Step 2 - 2 Minute Journaling: **What makes you feel powerful?**

Day 11

Step 1 - Step 1 - Read out loud to yourself your I AM statements & affirmations.

Step 2 - 2 Minute Journaling: **What do you want others to remember you for doing after you are gone?**

Day 12

Step 1 - Step 1 - Read out loud to yourself your I AM statements & affirmations.

Step 2 - 2 Minute Journaling: **What is the last compliment you received? How did you respond? How did it feel?**

Day 13

Step 1 - Step 1 - Read out loud to yourself your I AM statements & affirmations.

Step 2 - 2 Minute Journaling about: **the first thing you turn to when you feel sad or upset? Is it a healthy thing?**

Day 14

Step 1 - Step 1 - Read out loud to yourself your I AM statements & affirmations.

Step 2 - 2 Minute Journaling about: **activities that drain your energy the most?**

Day 15

Step 1 - Step 1 - Read out loud to yourself your I AM statements & affirmations.

Step 2 - 2 Minute Journaling about: **an activity that gives you an energy boost?**

Day 16

Step 1 - Step 1 - Read out loud to yourself your I AM statements & affirmations.

Step 2 - 2 Minute Journaling. Set your timer for 2 minutes and journal about... **someone that inspires you.**

Day 17

Step 1 - Step 1 - Read out loud to yourself your I AM statements & affirmations.

Step 2 - 2 Minute Journaling. Set your timer for 2 minutes and journal about...... **if success was guaranteed, what would you shoot for?**

Day 18

Step 1 - Step 1 - Read out loud to yourself your I AM statements & affirmations.

Step 2 - 2 Minute Journaling about: **something you have always wanted to do and yet time has slipped by without focusing on it.**

Day 19

Step 1 - Step 1 - Read out loud to yourself your I AM statements & affirmations.

Step 2 - 2 Minute Journaling about: **something that is a pet peeve for you and why do you feel/think you let it bother you?**

Day 20

Step 1 - Step 1 - Read out loud to yourself your I AM statements & affirmations.

Step 2 - 2 Minute Journaling..... **if YOU from 10 years in the future were to send you a letter thru time, what would it say?**

Day 21

Step 1 - Step 1 - Read out loud to yourself your I AM statements & affirmations.

Step 2 - 2 Minute Journaling...... **if money wasn't an issue, where would you want to live?**

Day 22

Step 1 - Step 1 - Read out loud to yourself your I AM statements & affirmations.

Step 2 - 2 Minute Journaling: **list as many people as you can think of that you appreciate having in your life.**

Day 23

Step 1 - Step 1 - Read out loud to yourself your I AM statements & Affirmations.

Step 2 - 2 Minute Journaling about...... **a dream that you need to put on hold for right now so you can pursue your purpose.**

Day 24

Step 1 - Step 1 - Read out loud to yourself your I AM statements & affirmations.

Step 2 - 2 Minute Journaling about...... **a boundary that you need to set for your own well-being.**

Day 25

Step 1 - Step 1 - Read out loud to yourself your I AM statements & affirmations.

Step 2 - 2 Minute Journaling about......**someone who has broken your trust and how it made you feel. What are you doing to let go of that past experience?**

Day 26

Step 1 - Step 1 - Read out loud to yourself your I AM statements & affirmations.

Step 2 - 2 Minute Journaling about......**something that felt like a bad experience when it happened that you now see as a blessing**

Day 27

Step 1 - Step 1 - Read out loud to yourself your I AM statements & affirmations.

Step 2 - 2 Minute Journaling about......**who is someone you compare yourself to sometimes and in which way.**

Day 28

Step 1 - Step 1 - Read out loud to yourself your I AM statements & affirmations.

Step 2 - 2 Minute Journaling about......**the last time you tried something new.**

Day 29

Step 1 - Step 1 - Read out loud to yourself your I AM statements & Affirmations.

Step 2 - 2 Minute Journaling about.....**something you wish you did more of 5 years ago.**

Day 30

Step 1 - Step 1 - Read out loud to yourself your I AM statements & affirmations.

Step 2 - 2 Minute Journaling: **Reflect on your last 30 days of focus & daily journaling. What positive impact have you noticed from it?**

You have completed 30 Days. Personal development and personal growth is an ongoing journey. I invite you to step up your game with a 90 Day Journey journal. Get your copy by scanning this QR code or go to

https://releaseyourinnerbadass.company.site/90-Day-Journey-p448184884

Daily Reminders

These are the pieces that were located on the inside jacket flaps of the original printing.

I AM Powerful beyond measure.
I HAVE all the strength I need.
I AM a light in the storm.
I AM in alignment with the great power.
I AM a gift.
I AM hope.
I AM unstoppable.
I AM joy.
I AM limitless.
I AM caring.
I AM love.
I AM peaceful.
I AM a creator.
I AM whole.
I AM a friend.
I AM a badass.

Everything can and will change.

You have overcome challenges before.

It's a learning experience.

Not getting what you want can be a blessing.

Allow yourself to have some fun.

Being kind to yourself is the best medicine.

Other people's negativity isn't with worrying about.

There is always, always, always, something to be Thankful for.

Special Video Message for you

Scan this QR code for a special video message,
or go to https://youtu.be/l-Z1fTJh8Vc

Marie-anne Rouse is a speaker, coach, best-selling author, and serial entrepreneur in the network marketing industry as well as the traditional business model. Her first books raised over 10K for natural disaster relief and after training with the legendary Les Brown, her writing and speaking have generated a different type of impact.

Originally from Europe, Marie-anne made her childhood dream a reality when she flew to Hawaii for her 19th birthday, moved there, and met the man who later became her husband. Besides loving to write, she loves to explore creative and artistic outlets such as playing with glitter, jewelry making, painting, and live theater both behind the scenes and on stage.

She is on a mission to inspire and motivate individuals whose nests have been shaken. She is on a mission to help them let go in order to live and soar. She is on a mission to help others Release their Inner Badass and find their own voice. She has done it herself, helped others do it and she can help you too.

For programs, books, freebies, and more:
LiveABetterWay.com